# A Sermon, Preached At The Dedication Of The First Congregational Church In New York

## Edward Everett

In the interest of creating a more extensive selection of rare historical book reprints, we have chosen to reproduce this title even though it may possibly have occasional imperfections such as missing and blurred pages, missing text, poor pictures, markings, dark backgrounds and other reproduction issues beyond our control. Because this work is culturally important, we have made it available as a part of our commitment to protecting, preserving and promoting the world's literature. Thank you for your understanding.

A

# SERMON,

PREACHED AT

## THE DEDICATION

OF THE

## FIRST CONGREGATIONAL CHURCH

IN

## NEW YORK,

*Jan. 20, 1821.*

BY EDWARD EVERETT.

PUBLISHED BY REQUEST OF THE SOCIETY.

Second Edition.

BOSTON:
PUBLISHED BY CUMMINGS AND HILLIARD, NO. 1 CORNHILL,
AND OLIVER EVERETT, NO. 6 COURT-STREET.
Univ. Press—Hilliard & Metcalf.
1821.

US 15597.83.25

Nov 26, 1917

Winslow Lewis tracts
New England Historic Genealogical Society

# SERMON.

2 CHRON. ii. 4.

*Behold, I build an house to the name of the Lord my God, to dedicate it to him.*

No practice is more consonant to reason, or confirmed by examples of greater antiquity and weight, than that of solemnly dedicating the places of religious worship to the honour and service of its object. Mankind in all ages, and under all forms alike of true or false religion, have transferred something of the sanctity of religious worship to the places where it is performed; and have felt the decency and propriety of separating them, by a solemn act of consecration, from every secular use or association, and devoting them to the Great Being, for whose service they were built. The sacred history, in that passage from which the text is taken, relates with precision the magnificent pomp with which the temple of Solomon was dedicated; and records, in other parts, the zeal and devotion with which the remnant of the captivity sought to emulate, in the latter house, the well remembered glory of the former. Nor were the ancient heathen less observant of this act of religious duty. Their temples were solemnly devoted to the gods; and once consecrated, they became, by a tenderness of religious feeling, which might have been imitated by Christians, sacred and inviolate; nor could they afterwards, by any change of appropriation, pass to a secular use, without the crime of sacrilege.*

We are assembled, Brethren of this Church, Christian Friends, to perform this interesting and solemn act—formally, to dedicate and devote to God, and to his worship, this house which, with his providential aid, you have erected; we have come to pray that he would crown our labours with his blessing; that he would vouchsafe his presence in the house which we have built; that he would record his name on the altar which we have set up; and that, while we have thus built him an earthly house with hands, he would so edify and build up our hearts in the faith of the

* The following principles, from the Institutes, are well known to have been derived, as the passage itself intimates, from the Ante-Justinianean law:

Sacræ res sunt, quæ rite per pontifices Deo consecratæ sunt, veluti ædes sacræ, et donaria quæ rite ad ministerium Dei dedicata sunt, quæ etiam per nostram constitutionem alienari et obligari prohibuimus, excepta causa redemptionis captivorum. Locus autem in quo ædes sacræ sunt ædificatæ *etiam diruto ædificio,* sacer adhuc manet, ut et Papinianus scripsit. Inst. II. 1. 8.

Gospel, that we may hereafter be found worthy to worship him, in that house not made with hands, eternal and on high.

"Behold, I build an house to the name of the Lord my God, to dedicate it to him." These are the words of the pious king of Israel: they should also be ours. We build an house to the Lord our God, to dedicate it to him. We dedicate our house,

1. To God.

To no earthly power, to no human name; but to God, who reigns on high. It is henceforth not ours, but his: we resign, devote, and consecrate it to him; and over its portal we would inscribe in our hearts, *Holiness to the Lord*. But,

2. This is not an empty and formal offering; we have not erected an unprofitable monument, as if the Almighty could be pleased with the tribute of a useless work of art. The temple we have built is not like the splendid structures of the ancient world, a merely votive edifice to the honour of the Divinity, who was thought to delight in the pomp and grandeur of the pile which bore his name. We dedicate our temple to the *worship* of God; and we would devote, at his mercy-seat, the most precious offering in our power to bestow;—a structure, which owes all its worth and importance to the religious ends it is to answer.

3. We dedicate this temple, not only as men, but as Christians; not only to God, the great First Cause, but to the God and Father of our Lord Jesus Christ. We dedicate it to the glorious cause of the Gospel. It is sacred henceforth to that alone. Let no other message be ever heard within its walls; no human science, no learning or art of this world; no cause or interest, which begins or ends with man; but the holy faith of the Son of God, and the truth as it is in Jesus.

4. Lastly, we dedicate it, in the liberty with which Christ has made us free, to the views we entertain of his Gospel and character. We dedicate it as Unitarians, not as a watchtower of polemic warfare, not as a gathering place for converts or proselytes; but that we may have the common privilege of worshipping God, according to the dictates of our own conscience, and enjoying that right which we cheerfully concede to others. We devote it to God the Father: We devote it to Christ his Son: We devote it to the Holy Spirit of grace and truth, with which we pray God, even now, to fill and sanctify us.

And now, my friends, before we are hurried on by the current of events, let us pause a moment to reflect upon the solemnity of an act like this, and to gather up and stamp upon our minds some of the feelings, which belong to us on the occasion.

No one but must allow, that the social character, and the social institutions of the Gospel, are among its most precious features. They are built on the sympathetic nature of man; they provide the means by which truth, instead of being confined to one, may be communicated; and goodness, personal as it necessarily is in itself, may be spread by advice and example. And without undervaluing the importance of secret discipline, of private prayer, of communion with our own hearts, and the searcher of our hearts, we may safely say, that it is to the social and public institutions of the Gospel, that its diffusion and preservation in the world are owing, under God. To the place, then, where these institutions are observed and celebrated; to the house where we assemble to join in praise and prayer, to confess our sins, and to ask Heaven's favours, to the spot from whence is dispensed to us the word of life, what solemn and tender associations must needs be attached. It is here, my friends, that you are henceforth to come to compare with each other your spiritual progress, to encourage each other in the Christian course. It is here you are to meet, not in the merciless ambition for office; not in the keen rivalry of gain; not in the empty interchange of courtesy; oh! not in the unholy emulation of vice: but where you are to meet to strengthen each other's good purposes; to animate each other's belief; to join your prayers and your praises; 'to take sweet counsel together.' It is here, if I do not mistake the views and feelings with which you have builded this house; if I do not too boldly hope for the divine blessing upon them; it is here that you are to spend some of the holiest and purest moments of your lives: hours redeemed from worldly care; seasons for the heart to rest, and the soul to breathe; it is here that there is the best hope, that those of you who are yet indifferent to your souls' salvation and eternal life, if any such there be, are to be awakened; here that God's praise is to come in its most solemn and affecting forms into your hearts; here that the embers of the heavenly fire are to be gathered and fanned into the glowing spirit of devotion. It is here, my brethren, if you are disposed to be good Christians, that you will strengthen and confirm, within these walls, the principles which are to direct, and the feelings which are to inspire you without them; and it is here that you are also to bring back the spirits bowed by the burdens, or wounded by the sins of life, and to ask for support or for pardon.

This is the great asylum—the place of refuge—the one spot left on earth, (blessed be God that one is left,) where business and pleasure cannot come; where the outward service of the world, at least, cannot enter; where, if you do not live for God, it is at least more immediately your own fault, without the palliation of pursuits, or appeals to distract you.—It is here that you are to perform some of the most interesting acts, and enter into the most solemn engagements; that you are to take upon you, as Providence may incline your hearts, the holy vows of the gospel, and meet from season to season at the table of the Lord to commemorate his dying love. Are you Christians, then, it is here that you will fulfil the most deliberate and solemn duties of Christian obedience. Are you parents? Scarcely will your children be given you, but you will be called to present them here, and record their name in the visible Church of Christ. Are you prosperous in life? You are here to offer your thanks. Are you unsuccessful? You are here to ask for support and comfort. You will find your hearts gathering themselves full fastly to these walls, and a thousand tender associations will bind you to them. Having here performed the public duties of Christians while you live, it is here, that when you are called away, the consolations of the Gospel will be supplicated by those who mourn for you. A few short years, and this new and tender interest will begin to arise in the hearts of husbands and wives, of parents and of children, of brothers and of sisters, who will here have brought the burden of their sorrows, in the most trying hours of life, and whose affections will come and dwell in these walls, with all that interest which belongs to the most tender and sacred associations. A few short years, and we shall all be gone; strangers, or at best our descendants, will stand in these places which we fill; but this house, which we have devoted to our Maker, will remain to give a spiritual continuity to our being. Those, who are to come after, will prize and love the spot where their parents worshipped. The last tie, which is severed in the pure and good heart, is that which binds it to the tombs and to the altars of its kindred; and if I do not mistake the providence which has hitherto directed you, generations unborn will repeat your names with interest and gratitude, as the founders of their church and their altar.

If sentiments like these give a tenderness to your minds, in performing this solemn act, there are others equally grave and interesting, which I ought not wholly to omit. I allude to that sense of responsibility, which you ought to feel from the peculiar circumstances under which you act on this occasion. You are dedicating a place of worship to the support of views of revealed truth, different, in some important points, from those of the respectable community in which you live; not extensively understood by your brethren and neighbours; or if understood, not regarded with favour. Under these circumstances, it is impossible that you should not be the objects of the prejudices, of the unfavourable opinions, of the opposition, with which whatever is thought new is apt to be regarded. You have only to put yourselves in the situation of your neighbours; and ask, what would be your prepossessions againt them, were you as great a majority in the community as you are a small minority, and you will feel that you have a claim to nothing but fairness and candour, and that it will be first necessary to establish your title to these, by showing that you deserve them. You can expect to conciliate the good opinion of worthy and pious men, not so much by the zeal with which you assert your views, as

1. By your personal characters for probity and worth. This is the first great argument by which you will win the hearts of the community, as it is the great test which our Lord himself proposed: " by their fruits ye shall know them." Do you wish to make people believe, that Unitarianism is a true doctrine; nothing will do it so effectually as showing that it makes its believers good men. The heart of prejudice itself cannot hold out against this. Be upright and honourable, punctual and trusty in the affairs of life: let your word and your promise be sure and faithful; your intercourse kind, friendly, and open: be not too forward, but always ready for every kind and charitable work: let your houses be the abode of decency

and of order, of purity and of peace: enter with moderation into the cheerful and innocent pleasures of life, for which Heaven has given us the senses, the faculties, and the tastes: build an altar of family worship in your dwellings; and be not superstitiously precise, but regular and punctual in your attendance on the public worship of this place, and you will need not to assert your claim to the name and character of Christians. You will require no ingenious defence of your tenets; you will not need the aid of learning and of eloquence; you will not need to ask for respect and charity: they will be more than paid, they will be given, they will be showered upon you. Your object, indeed, is not to make proselytes, but to save your own souls. Yet if it were your object to recommend your opinions to the adoption of others, the testimony of a pure, unspotted life, the outward operation of the inward faith, is the best and most persuasive missionary you can send into the world. This will convince those who will not be convinced by your reasons. For, as for reasons, and seemingly good reasons too, they may be had for almost any opinion; and error and truth are so mixed up in all the works of man, that there is scarce any doctrine of which much cannot be said in the defence, and much said in opposition; and above all, there is really so much which is true and good in every form of Christianity, as practised or held by sincere and worthy men, that of reason and argument there is really no end. I do not mean to say, that I do not think *our* views of Christianity rest on stronger foundations of argument, than any others essentially different. If I did not think so, I could not hold them and be an honest man. But you are Protestants—do you suppose that the great and ancient Catholic church, the church of Bossuet, of Massillon, of Fenelon, has no arguments by which those illustrious men were able to give a ground for their faith? Or you are Catholics—but do you think that Luther, and Calvin, and Melancthon, were led without strong and solid reasons to adopt what they called the Reformation? You are of the Church of England—but do you believe that Howe and Baxter had no arguments to defend their dissent? Or you are a Dissenter—but will you not allow that divines like Taylor and Tillotson had something to say for their cause? No, my friends, believe me, that the shortest and the most powerful argument by which you can enforce your claim to a fair standing in the Christian community is the witness of a pure heart, and the testimony of an unspotted life. But I will, notwithstanding, add, that you must unite with this claim that which belongs to

2. Serious, rational inquiry. To give a direction to this will be the duty of your future pastor, in his

public ministrations; but this will not exempt you in your individual capacities, from the duty of reading, reasoning, and judging, and still less from that of searching the scriptures, whether these things are so. Next to that claim to the public candour, which I have already enforced, will be that which you may ground on the reputation of the interest and diligence with which you pursue the study of divine truth. I do not mean that you should attempt to make yourselves professional theologians, for which, of course, they alone have time and leisure, who, as in every other profession, are set apart to the pursuit of this. But it is vain to pretend to any real interest in Christianity, if you do not take pains to inform yourselves of the evidences on which it rests, of the contents of the records, in which it is taught, and of the grounds on which your peculiar views of these records repose. Do you differ from your neighbours, and will you not hold yourselves ready to tell them why: do you think it your duty not to worship in their forms, or in their language, and will you not have some good reason to show for your own: do you rest your hope of divine mercy on different views of the Gospel, and will you not stand ready to account for the difference? Can you expect that you will be allowed even to be sincere and honest in your belief, if you are unable on proper time and occasion, and when properly called on, to show the foundations on which it is built? Or will not the credit allowed you for honesty, sincerity, and Christian standing, be rather in just proportion to the titles you are able to set up for your opinions, on grounds of plain fair reasoning, and uniform connected scriptural authority?

But should you unite these two claims to public charity and candour, viz. that of a blameless life, and of an inquiring temper, you will not long be deprived of your just place in the esteem of your neighbours, and you will be thought hardly of, only by those whose good opinion you would have no reason to covet. It will be seen, that for the common opprobrium which may be attached to your views there is no foundation. Persons, themselves of kind and good hearts, will find no difficulty in believing the honesty and uprightness of yours. Persons, of fair reflecting minds, will give your arguments an unprejudiced hearing. It will be seen, if by God's grace you will give it to be seen, that the doctrine you profess is a pure, a virtuous, and a holy doctrine. Men will not long believe, that with souls to save, you are deliberately sinning against your souls. If you studiously endeavour to adorn the doctrine of the Gospel, you will cease to be charged with wilfully corrupting it. If you are always ready to give a reason of the hope which is in you, fear not but that the fair and candid will do justice to it. Judicious men, used to tracing the springs of human character, the laws of evidence, and the grounds of action, will be able and be willing to do justice to your profession. Strange as the expression may seem, you will experience most charity from those who are most conscientiously opposed to you. No serious tender spirit, that prizes itself the infinite worth of religion, will be ready to suspect you of indifference to its value. No soul, on which the awe of God's presence has rested, will be forward to believe that you are playing a false or hollow part in his worship. No serious inquirer, who has wrestled himself with doubt, and has formed his own faith on deliberate and careful investigation, will unkindly question the honesty of your inquiries, because they have led you to a different result. Oh, no, my friends, fear not that justice will not be done you. Parents will look into their own hearts, and while they feel the strong and tender interest which binds them to their children, they will find it hard to believe that you are wantonly sacrificing not only your own salvation, but bringing up your sons and daughters to eternal ruin. Those whom Providence has visited with bereavement, and who have felt the unutterable worth of religious consolations in the hour of trial, will do justice to the sincerity of the faith which they see upholding you in yours. Let but your lives and characters be worthy of your profession, and you will have an advocate in every candid mind, in every warm heart, in every serious spirit, which will speak more loudly and persuasively for you, than all the learning, the wit, or the eloquence of the books.

But desirous as you, like all men, must be, to enjoy the good opinion of your neighbours, you must not dwell on that as a great and final object; nor forget that the ends, for which you have built this house, are higher and nobler, more solemn and momentous, than any thing this side of heaven. It is not your object to make proselytes, to extend your views, nor even to have them well spoken of by your neighbours; but to worship God according to the dictates of your conscience; to provide for the religious instruction of yourselves, your children, and your servants; and by the faithful and concientious observance of the appointed means of grace, prepare yourselves with fear and trembling for the great day of judgment and account. These are the objects you have in view in founding this church, and setting up this altar; great and eternal objects, weighed with which the favour or the opposition of man are lighter than the dust of the balance. You are to approve yourselves not to men, but to God: you are to be judged not by man, but by God: you are to seek and to gain not their favour, but His. I beseech you, therefore, brethren, to watch and pray against a polemic or controversial spirit. The soul of devotion expires beneath it. Let not your anxiety to correct the erroneous views which may be entertained of your doctrine, betray you out of the sanctuary of a pure, humble, self-communing, and self-searching temper, into the walks of disputation and controversy. Find, if it may be, that happy medium between an unbecoming acquiescence, and a jealous championship; and while you withhold not your testimony to the truth, as in your hearts and souls you hold and believe it:—think, I pray you, and feel, that as it is better even to err in speculation and be pious in spirit, than to speak heavenly truths with lips of bitterness; so it is incomparably, unspeakably better to bear misrepresentations with meekness, than to meet them with passion. Your judge and witness is on high, who is able to search out your cause, and of whose pure and holy religion the soul and the essence is love.

Lastly, my brethren, there is one more consideration, which naturally offers itself on this occasion, and which I do not feel at liberty to pass over. The circumstances in which, as a religious society, you are placed, will render you a sort of model and exemplar of the doctrine you profess in a community, second to none in our country for extent and respectability.

Do you consider that doctrine as all important: do you think that it involves high and honourable views of the divine character and government: that it teaches the Gospel in its most affecting form, and is eminently favourable to the purity and elevation of the human mind and of the human heart?—and can you look upon it as a small responsibility, that the estimation in which such a doctrine is held, and the progress it makes in a community, in many respects already, and destined, perhaps, to be in all the metropolis of our country, depends on you? It is not then the concerns of your own little flock, or the church you are founding, that are entrusted to you, but the cause of liberal Christianity in this portion of the American Zion. If you stand worthily this test, you will promote, I say not your own interests; I greatly err if that be a motive which predominates in your minds; but you will promote the great cause to which you are devoted; you will do honour to the pure and elevated conceptions of divine truth you have embraced; and advance the kingdom of the Master, by whose name you are called. If you stand worthily this test, you will not only rejoice the spirits of those who have gone before you in the same profession, but you will strengthen the hands and encourage the hearts of thousands of devout and timid Christians, who will gladly come and join you, while, in the words of Bishop Hoadley, you "celebrate a solemn marriage between Reason and Faith." And, oh, my friends, if you fail; if the light which I devoutly persuade myself has been kindled by Heaven, should coldly expire on the altar; if the zeal of a small and forming association grow cool with prosperity; if the great objects of your own salvation, and that of your children, be forgotten, for any meaner end; if the high and holy cause of spiritual liberty and free inquiry should suffer and be spoken ill of in your hands, then you will offend not against yourselves alone, who were called to a higher vocation; not against your children alone, whom you will defraud of their just inheritance of instruction and truth; not against the community, whose eyes are upon you, and whose hopes you will have disappointed and betrayed; but against all throughout Christendom, who share your convictions; against all those pious Pastors and faithful Churches of Christ, who, throughout our native land, are bearing you on their prayers to Heaven. You will offend against all the witnesses to the cause of truth, who, with whatever different views, have laboured, and suffered, and bled in the same great cause of the rights of conscience and the freedom of inquiry. You will offend against the venerable exiles, who brake the yoke of the English church, and clung fast to the standard of private judgment, yea, when it was planted amidst icy storms, on the iron-bound coasts of the north. You will offend against that illustrious church of England itself, which hastened, in the dawn of the reformation, to throw off the Papal yoke, and which would no more demand of you blindly to adopt their creed, than they did that of their fathers. You will offend against the first, who sounded the trumpet of the Reformation;—against Luther, and Calvin, and Zuingli, " great men of God," as the pious Robinson said of one of them, " who yet saw not all things," but who saw one thing plain and clear, that they would call no man Master but Christ. You will offend against that reason which is the candle of the Lord : you will offend against that understanding which is the inspiration of the Almighty : you will prepare another most unholy triumph for all who have hated light and truth since the world began ; and not a child of darkness but will start to greet you from below, and fiercely cry, ' art thou become like unto us !'

Let not your hearts, my friends, sink, as though oppressed by this great responsibility. Think not that you stand unaided and solitary in the world. Do not suppose that you are alone, even in the community where you dwell. He that is not against you is for you; and the greatest part of your neighbours will do you justice, and wish you well. You cannot ask that they should leave their churches, and desert their pastors, to join you; it is enough that they bear you Christian charity, and give you credit for Christian sincerity. You are not alone, for the views of Christianity you profess already prevail extensively in some of our most respectable communities, and are rapidly spreading in others; and not an effort will you make, nor a prayer will you offer, but will find an echo in many a church, where the candlestick of the Lord hath been lighted from the first. You are not alone, my brethren; sincerity and piety are never alone: you are not alone, for the Father is with you. He is with all of all communions, who seek and serve him. May we not humbly hope that he is even here; that the gracious presence, which is extended to all the dwellings of the just, is more especially vouchsafed to the temples where his honour dwelleth. This is none other than the house of God, the gate of heaven.

Brethren, but one word more and I have done. Except the Lord build the house, they labour in vain who build it. If this church is founded on private feeling or worldly zeal, or has been erected from any motive of human interest, then not the Lord, but you have built it, and you have most assuredly laboured in vain. But if it is erected on the faith and hope of the Gospel; if it is consecrated in your hearts to the glory of God, and the purity of the truth as it is in Jesus; if you have built upon the foundation of the

Prophets and Apostles, Jesus Christ himself being the chief corner stone, then not you, but the Lord hath builded:—then you are founded on a rock, that shall not be moved:—then, though the rains descend, and the floods come, and the winds blow, you cannot fall:—then will your church be recorded among the strong watchtowers of the Gospel:—the Lord will plant his banner over you, which is love; and so long as that shall float above your sanctuary, the gates of hell will not prevail against it.

Printed by Libri Plureos GmbH in Hamburg, Germany